Weather Central

Also by Ted Kooser

Sure Signs: New and Selected Poems, 1980

One World at a Time, 1985

Weather Central

Ted Kooser

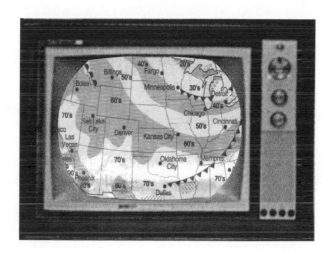

University of Pittsburgh Press
Pittsburgh • London

The publication of this book is supported by a grant from the Pennsylvania Council on the Arts.

Published by the University of Pittsburgh Press, Pittsburgh, Pa. 15261
Copyright © 1994, Ted Kooser
All rights reserved
Manufactured in the United States of America
Printed on acid-free paper
10 9 8 7 6 5 4 3

Library of Congress Cataloging-in-Publication Data

Kooser, Ted.
    Weather central / Ted Kooser.
        p.   cm. —(Pitt Poetry Series)
    ISBN 0-8229-3796-4 (cl.).—ISBN 0-8229-5527-X (pbk.)
    I. Title.   II. Series.
PS3561.06W43   1994   94-11758
811'.54—dc20   CIP

A CIP catalogue record for this book is available from the British Library.

Eurospan, London

The author and publisher wish to express their grateful acknowledgment to the following publications in which some of these poems first appeared: *The Antioch Review* ("Ditch-burning in February"); *Arete* ("Another Story" formerly "A Story"); *Borderlands* ("A Hatch of Flies"); *The Cream City Review* ("Fireflies," "A Ghost Story," "A Letter in October," "Nocturne," "Pasture Trees," "The Sweeper"); *Fine Madness* ("An Epiphany," "Oceans of Fun," "Old Dog in March," "Site"); *Madison Review* ("Shoes"); *Nebraska English Journal* ("Chocolate Checkers," "Home Storage Barns," "Yevtushenko"); *Nebraska Humanities* ("An Elegy," "The Time of Their Lives"); *The North Dakota Quarterly* ("A Good-bye Handshake," "Sparklers," "A Statue of the Unknown Soldier," "A Stoneware Crock"); *Northeast Corridor* ("Night Class," "Skywalk"); *Poetry East* ("The Mouse in the Piano"); *Poetry Northwest* ("City Limits"); *Prairie Schooner* ("An Abandoned Stone Schoolhouse in the Nebraska Sandhills," "Barn Owl," "Five Finger Exercise," "In Late Spring," "In Passing," "The Little Hats," "Poem Before Breakfast," "A Poetry Reading," "A Sound in the Night"); *Southern Poetry Review* ("Spider Eggs"); *Swamp Root* ("In a Kitchen Garden"); *Three Rivers Poetry Journal* ("A Finding," "The Gilbert Stuart Portrait of Washington"); and *Wisconsin Review* ("The Great Grandparents," "Lincoln, Nebraska" formerly "Nebraska Baedecker").

"The Back Door" and "Snakeskin" first appeared in *The Hudson Review*.

"Surveyors" and "Weather Central" were first published in *The Kenyon Review*—New Series, Fall 1992, Vol. XIV, No. 4.

Book design: Frank Lehner

for my mother and my sister

Contents

Weather Central

Etude

I have been watching a Great Blue Heron
fish in the cattails, easing ahead
with the stealth of a lover composing a letter,
the hungry words looping and blue
as they coil and uncoil, as they kiss and sting.

Let's say that he holds down an everyday job
in an office. His blue suit blends in.
Long days swim beneath the glass top
of his desk, each one alike. On the lip
of each morning, a bubble trembles.

No one has seen him there, writing a letter
to a woman he loves. His pencil is poised
in the air like the beak of a bird.
He would spear the whole world if he could,
toss it and swallow it live.

1

In Late Spring

One of the National Guard's F-4 jet fighters,
making a long approach to the Lincoln airfield,
comes howling in over the treetops, its shadow
flapping along behind it like the skin of a sheep,
setting the coyotes crying back in the woods,
and then the dogs, and then there is a sudden quiet

that rings a little, the way an empty pan
rings when you wipe it dry, and then it is
Sunday again, a summer Sunday afternoon,
and beyond my window, the Russian Olives
sigh foolishly into the air through the throats of their
          flowers,
and bluegills nibble the clouds afloat on the pond.

Under the windmill, a cluster of peonies huddles,
bald-headed now, and standing in piles of old papers.
Beneath its lipstick, the mouth of the tulip is twisted.
Spring moves on, on her run-down broken toe shoes
into the summer, trailing green ribbons of silk.

I have been reading for hours, or intending to read,
but over the bee-song of the book I could faintly hear
my neighbor up the road a quarter mile
calling out to his daughter, and hear her calling back,
not in words but in musical notes, and now that they
have fallen quiet, and I have listened long into their absence,
I have forgotten my place in the world.

But the world knows my place and stands and holds a chair
for me, here on these acres near Garland, Nebraska.
This April, in good health, I entered my fifty-fourth year.
The perfect porcelain bells of Lily-of-the-Valley
ring into the long, shy ears of the ferns,
and the horsefly sits in the sun and twirls his mustache
and brushes the dust from his satin sleeves.

A Finding

One of my dogs has brought the foreleg of a deer
up from the bottom woods, and gnawed on it a while,
and left it next to the door like a long-stemmed rose,
the joint at its shoulder red and flowering
where the dog has neatly licked the earth away.

Often they die like that, gut-shot by a hunter
or carrying an arrow for miles. I've found their bones
up under banks where they've hidden in caves of roots,
curled themselves over their pain, and kicked at the
    coyotes.
And the dogs have found far more of them than I.

Picking it up, a delicate life runs lightly
over my hands. The knee-joint's smooth articulation
folds the leg into itself like a carpenter's rule.
There's a spring to these bones, the hair laid back from
    flying,
the hoof like a castanet ready to clatter.

The wind lifts just a little, gets in under the fur,
and I see on the shin a tiny, tar black scar
from a barbed-wire fence leapt not so long ago.
My two dogs stand and look out over the fields,
and the three of us can hear that wire still thrumming.

A Hatch of Flies

There are more than a hundred
buzzing against the scummy glass
of the window, trying to break out
of the wintry barn into the first
warm day of the year, most of them
walking in circles over the solid
sunlight, angry, some of them silent,
tapping the milky, dusty glass
with their forelegs, apparently
thinking. Two species of housefly,
one shrill and black, the other
larger and slower, with a touch of green
on its back, precisely the color
of a sunny hillside on a day
like this, new grass pushing up
out of the brown. All perfectly made,
with black parts joined like lengths
of stovepipe, brains like spark plugs;
some of each species thinkers,
some of each movers and shakers,
some merely pushing and screaming,
a couple of each locked motionless
in sex, the female firm as a table
under the male, the male astounded,
touching his eyes with his tiny hands.

An Elegy

In summer, after the spring floods
have fallen away, there are always
the thin, girlish leaves of the willows
left by the river to dry—
draped over tangles of driftwood,
thrown over the roots of old trees—
their greenness gone, their ribs and webbing
spun into a thick, dull paper
upon which all the words have run together,
whatever they said. But you must know
that the field mouse now finds shelter there,
and the leopard frog who sings all night,
and the water strider setting out
across the water, long-legged and light
as a breath.

Snakeskin

It is only the old yellow shell
of something long gone on,
a dusty tunnel echoing
with light, yet you can feel
the speed along it, feel
in your bones the tick of wheels.

You hold a glove of lace,
a loose glitter of sequins.
The ghost of a wind is in it still
for someone only yesterday
was waving it: good-bye.

Somewhere, a long train
crosses a border. The sun lights lamps
in its thousand round windows.
All it knows is behind it already.
Nothing it knows is ahead.
Its whistle flicks into the distance.

Poem Before Breakfast

A small brown bird flies toward me
over the pond, ferrying light
on its back, on its gliding wings,
bearing up part of the morning,

a small brown part—merely a flake
of significance, really, in all
the world of light around it,
blue, yellow, and green, yet

perfectly cared for, perfectly
tended, one piece of a moment
borne skillfully over the water,
and I blessed to receive it.

Fireflies

The cricket's pocketknife is bent
from prying up the lid of a can
of new moons. It skips on the grindstone,
chattering, showering sparks
that float away over the darkened yard.

This is the Fourth of July
for the weary ants, who have no union,
who come home black with coal dust.
Deep in the grass you can hear them
unfolding their canvas chairs.

There is a pier that arches out
into the evening, its pilings of shadow,
its planking of breeze, and on it
a woman stands snapping the shade
of a lantern, signaling someone.

The Time of Their Lives

Today my ducks are eating windfalls
under the broken Jonathan tree—
nine white Pekins laughing like nuns
on a picnic, rolling the apples around
in the grass with their orange bills,
having the time of their lives.

Nothing escapes them. Near them,
a red leaf rides the long grass
with a papery rattle. A sweat-bee
deep in an apple sucks
the tart cider. A lacy elm leaf
sifts the wind. Their black eyes sparkle.

There is already ice in the reeds
at the edge of the pond. I have built
a cage in the dark garage, for tomorrow
they go to a hard young farm wife
easy with killing. They will be
packaged like gifts, heavy as hearts.

Their cage is sturdy, quick to close.
As my hammer tapped, they arched their necks
to hear better the tick of scales
as a bull snake passed. Above the cry
of my table saw, they heard a hawk's wings
dust the blue bowl of the sky.

A Letter in October

Dawn comes later and later now,
and I, who only a month ago
could sit with coffee every morning
watching the light walk down the hill
to the edge of the pond and place
a doe there, shyly drinking,

then see the light step out upon
the water, sowing reflections
to either side—a garden
of trees that grew as if by magic—
now see no more than my face,
mirrored by darkness, pale and odd,

startled by time. While I slept,
night in its thick winter jacket
bridled the doe with a twist
of wet leaves and led her away,
then brought its black horse with harness
that creaked like a cricket, and turned

the water garden under. I woke,
and at the waiting window found
the curtains open to my open face;
beyond me, darkness. And I,
who only wished to keep looking out,
must now keep looking in.

2

Lincoln, Nebraska

Rainy today in this city
the color of pigeons, this gray
rail-town tucked under
the shadowy heave and clang
of its iron bridges,

city nested on ledges
runny with lime; old rail-head
with lice in its wings
and a broken beak, its eggs
all gone to vinegar.

Thin rain has all day rinsed
a chain-link fence
with a high-heeled slipper
snapped off in its face,
and moistened the torn

red lips of a purse
stuffed under a loading dock.
A clump of prairie grass
spattered with creosote
stands next to the rails

like the last scalp-lock
of the last Pawnee,
like the last black cough
of the bison. Yet there
is something beautiful

about a dirty town in rain,
where tin cans, rails,
and toppled shopping carts
are the sutures of silver
holding the guts in,

keeping the blue wound closed,
while over a pawnshop, the plain
wet flag of a yellow window
holds out the cautious welcome
of an embassy.

A Heart of Gold

It's an old beer bottle
with a heart of gold. There's a lot
of defeat in those shoulders,
sprinkled with dandruff, battered
by years of huddling up
with good buddies, out of the wind.

This is no throwaway bottle.
Full of regret and sad stories,
here it comes, back into your life
again and again, ready to stand
in front of everyone you know
and let you peel its label off.

Now, from the wet formica tabletop,
it lifts its sweet old mouth to yours.

Oceans of Fun

A man on his back comes bumping down
the water slide, eyes closed, his white hands
crossed on his breast. His wife and daughter
wait in the pool at the bottom, bobbing
in billowy gooseflesh and gaudy suits
as down and down his shiny body races,
throwing out delicate, glittering wings.
We cannot read the woman's wet face
through the spatter of light, nor the tight
white features of the girl, who rocks up
onto her toes and covers her mouth
as her father flies past, sliding out onto
the thin blue ice of the air. For an instant
he floats there, composed, and all of us
float there beside him, holding our breath,
weightless and free. Let us leave our scene
there, with all of us wet and alive
in the air over Kansas, the sun's warmth
reaching all the way into our bones,
our loved ones looking up and by so doing
somehow holding us there while beneath us
the earth rolls east—whipping the blue pool
to whitecaps, bending the manicured grasses—
at more than a thousand miles an hour.

The Little Hats

I saw the old men hanging down under their little hats
as the hats pulled them stumbling along—
those polyester hats with little checkers,
with little feathers, yellow and red—
and their eyes were wide behind their shiny glasses,
and their cries pinched off and blue.

And when they had passed, and the bitter squeal
of their cane tips braking had faded,
I saw there in the enormous window
of the secondhand store, cast off, a row of little hats,
streamlined and swift, their engines idling.

Four Secretaries

All through the day I hear or overhear
their clear, light voices calling
from desk to desk, young women whose fingers
play casually over their documents,

setting the incoming checks to one side,
the thick computer reports to the other,
tapping the correspondence into stacks
while they sing to each other, not intending

to sing nor knowing how beautiful
their voices are as they call back and forth,
singing their troubled marriage ballads,
their day-care, car-park, landlord songs.

Even their anger with one another
is lovely: the color rising in their throats,
their white fists clenched in their laps,
the quiet between them that follows.

And their sadness—how deep and full of love
is their sadness when one among them
is hurt, and they hear her calling
and gather about her to cry.

A Blind Woman

She had turned her face up into
a rain of light, and came on smiling.

The light trickled down her forehead
and into her eyes. It ran down

into the neck of her sweatshirt
and wet the white tops of her breasts.

Her brown shoes splashed on
into the light. The moment was like

a circus wagon rolling before her
through puddles of light, a cage on wheels,

and she walked fast behind it,
exuberant, curious, pushing her cane

through the bars, poking and prodding,
while the world cowered back in a corner.

Chocolate Checkers

In a tiny green park, chopped out
of a corner of Commerce, I saw
two men in rags with their backpacks
lying beside them. Red nose to red nose
and old boots toe to toe, they were
playing a game of chocolate checkers,
using candy for pieces, and eating
the pieces they'd won from each other
and laughing like crazy.
                              It was Commerce
who'd given this park to the city,
and Commerce looked on—the bank
and the telephone company
standing behind mirrored windows,
disapproving—not of chocolate checkers
per se, but of that kind of people,
laughing and playing with candy
on an imported Italian marble table
with neatly set black-and-white tiles.

Night Class

An autumn evening, dry leaves
up on their sharp little hooves
and galloping out of the way
of the traffic, streetlights
touching the yellow petticoats
of trees, a rich blue darkness
over the campus, and a girl
in a white nylon jacket
crossing the hour like a moon.

All this beyond a classroom
bright and sour as an empty carton
of vanilla ice cream, where
a teacher and his dozen students
surround their words, drawing
their chairs up into a circle,
dangling their legs in the pit
where poems fly at each other
with blades on their spurs.

On a wall, a dusty chalkboard
covered with scratches: a lens
through which the great leviathan
of the Tradition peers,
slowly fanning its bony fins,
its gills scarcely moving,
eyes milky with cataracts,
its hard jaw bruised and scarred
from bumping the cold green glass.

The girl who is the moon
passes below their lighted window,
a trace of cigarette smoke

in her hair, Juicy Fruit sweet
on her breath. The poets know
nothing of her, nor she of them.
She wears a kiss behind her ear,
the left one, in the hollow there
through which a pale light glows.

Shoes

In the shoe store storage closet,
the smooth brown eggs of new shoes
lie glowing in boxes, nestled
in christening gowns, their eyelets
already open and staring
but their laces still tightly folded
in dark little fists. Let us
not tell them just yet
that they will all too soon
be just like the others, waiting in rank
by size and sex and color
at the secondhand store—
old shoes with cracked faces,
with sore hands fanned out on their knees,
their toes turned up from forever
walking uphill in the rain.

A Deck of Pornographic Playing Cards

We were ten or eleven, my friend and I,
when we found them up under a bridge,
on top of a beam where pigeons were resting.
Someone had carefully hidden them there.
On each was a black-and-white photo,
no two cards alike. We grew quiet and older,
young men on our haunches, staring at
what we feared might be the future.
The pigeons flapped back to their roosts,
rustling and cooing. The river gurgled
as it slipped from the bridge's cool shadow.
There were women with big muzzled dogs,
women with bottles and broom handles.
Stallions stood over the bodies of others.
The women smiled and licked their lips
with tongues like thorns. We grew old.
We were two old men with stiff legs
and sad hearts. We had wanted to laugh
but we couldn't. We had thought we were boys,
come there to throw stones at the pigeons,
but we were already dying inside.

Baseball

The batter pushes his way through the light
like a diver walking the floor of the sea.
He kicks up a glowing green dust
that trails from his ankles in flowing ribbons.

At the plate, he positions his feet
and his buoyant shoulders shrug and settle.
His elbows lift and fall as if his body
were the mouth of something slowly breathing.

He stirs the thick hours with his bat.

The pitcher turns on his stem, a wavering blade
of sea grass. His soft white hand floats up
and bumps the black bill of his cap.

The ball comes out of his arm like a bubble.

The batter swings slowly, and when he connects,
that muffled clack is one tick of the clock.
It will be days before we hear another.

Skywalk

It bridges the busy street, building to building,
like an enormous cocoon, spun out
between one nowhere and the next, and in it
tight knots of teenaged boys in leather skins
press out against its walls, working their
mandibles, breathing the stream of air,
their faces tight and impatient and sore,
each waiting for his stiff black shell to split
and his beautiful wings to unfold.

Yevtushenko

Yevtushenko, you came to Nebraska.
Yes, of all places, Nebraska—
cornfield, wheatfield, cow, and college.

You had a sore throat, and you smelled of camphor.
Your blue eyes were small in your face.

You read your windy poems, Yevtushenko,
like a tree in the wind you read them,
waving your branches. We sat back
as far in our seats as we could,
frightened of Russia. Then it was over
and you scooped up your leaves and sat down.

After the party, we drove across town
to the Governor's house. It was already late.
You wanted to sit in the Governor's chair
and he let you. You drank his red wine
and showed us the long movie you'd made
of your life. You recited a list of the people
you knew: Kissinger, Nixon, Kennedy (Bob).

The Governor's eyes were as hollow as Lincoln's.
He nodded as Lincoln must have nodded
while Mary Todd Lincoln went over the menu.
At three in the morning, we finally left,
and when you thanked him, Yevtushenko, for his time,
he said it was all part of the job.

In Passing

From a half block off I see you coming,
walking briskly along, carrying parcels,
furtively glancing up into the faces
of people approaching, looking for someone
you know, holding your smile in your mouth
like a pebble, keeping it moist and ready,
being careful not to swallow.

I know that hope so open on your face,
know how your heart would lift to see just one
among us who remembered. If only someone
would call out your name, would smile,
so happy to see you again. You shift
your heavy parcels, hunch up your shoulders,
and press ahead into the moment.

From a few feet away, you recognize me,
or think you do. I see you preparing your face,
getting your greeting ready. Do I know you?
Both of us wonder. Swiftly we meet and pass,
averting our eyes, close enough to touch,
but not touching. I could not let you know
that I've forgotten, and yet you know.

A Poetry Reading

Once you were young along a river, tree to tree,
with sleek black wings and red shoulders.
You sang for yourself but all of them listened to you.

Now you're an old blue heron with yellow eyes
and a gray neck tough as a snake.
You open your book on its spine, a split fish,
and pick over the difficult ribs,
turning your better eye down to the work
of eating your words as you go.

City Limits

Here on the west edge, the town turned its back on the
    west,
gave up the promise, nodded good-bye to a highway
that narrowed away, and with a sunset-red bandanna
bid the shimmering tracks go on, go on.

Go west, young man, cheered Horace Greeley, and west
rattled the new country, rocking along through the sparks,
the cattle dying, the children sick, the limits
always ahead like a wall of black mountains.

But the steam cooled and condensed, the pistons rusted.
The dead weight of trunks thudded onto the platform,
bursting their leather straps. Generations spilled out
and we settled for limits: strung fence wire, drew plat maps

with streets squared to the polestar, passed finicky laws,
built churches true: the bubble centered in the spirit level.
We let the plumb bob swing till it stopped with its point
on the spot where we were, where we were to remain.

The frontier rolled on ahead; we never caught up
with whatever it was, that rolling wave or weather front,
those wings of cloud. The news came back, delivered by
    failure,
a peach-crate of rags, a face caved in over its smiles.

We thrived on the failure of others; rich gossip
flowered like vines on the trellises. On porches,
what once had been dream leaned back on its rockers.
We could have told them. We could have told them so.

The bean-strings ran back and forth through the vines
defining our limits. Children played by the rules:
cat's cradle, Red Rover. Morticians showed up
with wagons of markers. The dead lay in their places.

Our horses grew heavy and lame tied to pickets
and our wheel-rims rusted and sprang from their spokes.
Fire-pit became city, its flashing red pennants strung
over the car lot. We signed on the line at the bank.

What we'd done to the Indians happened to us.
Our hearts had never been in it, this stopping;
we wanted a nowhere but gave ourselves over to gardens.
Now our old campsite limits itself on the west

to the lazy abandon of sunset—a pint bottle
whistling the blues in a dry prairie wind. Next to
the tracks, turning first one way and then another,
a switch with red eyes wipes its mouth with a sleeve.

The Gilbert Stuart Portrait
of Washington

You know it as well as the back of your hand,
that face like a blushing bouquet
of pink peonies set in the shadows of war,
the father of our country, patient,
sucking the past from his wooden teeth.

His famous portrait, never completed,
hung on the wall at the front of the classroom
next to a black octagonal clock
with the ghost of a teacher trapped inside,
tapping out time with a piece of chalk.

It was easy to see his attention
was elsewhere. He'd left a dozen campfires
burning out there at the front of his face,
then retreated behind them. At fifty-eight,
he was old and broken. This was no way

to use up the days of a soldier.
Celebrity irked him. He had little time
for the likes of Gilbert Stuart, that son
of a snuff-grinding Tory, that slackard
who sat out the war with the English.

Perched on a chair in a cold stone barn,
according to Stuart, he smiled only once,
when a stallion ran past. He cared more
for thoroughbred horses and farming
than he did for the presidency.

On the wall between us and the future,
at the point where all of the lines converged,

George Washington, like any other man,
suppressed a deep sigh. So heavy was life;
how futile it seemed to protest.

We learned our lessons while the big clock
clacked, its Roman numerals arranged
in a wreath and sealed under glass. Those were
lovely calico autumns; then winter passed
with its long, clean pennants of light;

then spring with its chaffy rustle. We thought
those aisles were parallel, that our days
would never arrive at the vanishing point.
Before us always, he who could never tell a lie
kept his jaws closed on the truth.

3

Site

A fenced-in square of sand and yellow grass,
five miles or more from the nearest town
is the site where the County Poor Farm stood
for seventy years, and here the County
permitted the poor to garden, permitted them
use of the County water from a hand-pump,
lent them buckets to carry it spilling
over the grass to the sandy, burning furrows
that drank it away—a kind of Workfare
from 1900. At night, each family slept
on the floor of one room in a boxy house
that the County put up and permitted them
use of. It stood here somewhere, door
facing the road. And somewhere under this grass
lie the dead in the County's unmarked graves,
each body buried with a mason jar in which
each person's name is written on a paper.
The County provided the paper and the jars.

Ditch-burning in February

Driving, I came to a mile of fire
running like blood by a country road.
I slowed in the smoke as flames seeped
through weeds, soaked fence posts,
and splashed over into a field.

A man about my age stood ankle-deep
there in the shallows, hanging his weight
on a long-handled spade, pressing
the wood to his cheek. As he leaned
on his shovel, I leaned on the wheel.

As I passed, I could feel that cold shaft
in my hands and an ache in my shoulders.
He lifted a finger to wave, and I
waved back. His smoke rolled out over
the fields like a season, like spring.

Behind his fire lay last year's tossed-out
bottles, gleaming like milestones. Ahead,
the road ran on, bordered by weeds.
I watched him go east in the mirror,
and he watched me go west and away.

An Abandoned Stone Schoolhouse
in the Nebraska Sandhills

These square stone walls are of sand, too:
blocks of cut sandstone, stone yet sand

like all sands, always ready to go,
always showing their glittering sails.

Someday, with the work of the wind,
this will all be gone—the hollow school,

its hollow in the changing hills,
the fallen door with its shiny black knob.

Touch the wall with your fingertips,
and a hundred thousand years brush away

just like that, exposing no more
than a faint stain the color of coffee.

Put your palm flat on these stones.
Something is happening under the surface:

even in sunlight, the stone feels cool,
as if water were trickling inside,

flowing through darkness—a silent,
shadowy river, cleaning itself

as it eases along through the sand,
rubbing away at our names and our voices.

Pasture Trees

Generations of cows, long gone to market
fat and forlorn, once lipped the lowest leaves
and nibbled the lower limbs until these old

box elder trees are level as thunderheads
across their bases, showering shadows
into the long, lush grass, a rain of absence

pattering flat on the hard-packed cow path
turning toward home, toward the hilltop barn
that fell away, that followed the cattle

lowing into the past, its creaking slats
sore-sided as a rack of wet alfalfa
from laboring under the weight of weather;

that steamy barn that hid the rising sun
as the cows walked slowly out into the world
every morning like widows leaning on air;

that stark, black silhouette that for a moment
each evening held the galvanized pail
of the moon tipped under the bony elbow

of an eave—a dented moon that slowly filled
with milk for the many who lived here then:
happy, unhappy: young people and old

who borrowed bitterly to own those creatures
who danced all day on their back legs, stretching
to eat the very trees that gave them shade.

The Lost Forge

It stood somewhere in summer,
under a rusty tin roof
that showered sparks of afternoon
over the shadows—a well
of charred and crumbling brick
brim full of emptiness
from which some farmer once
had ladled bowls of flame
and dipped his tools in light.

Over that oily, joyless dirt,
he'd sprinkled molten iron
that cooled to a carpet of clover
rusty with autumn, and to fingery
oak leaves reaching through time.

I stood at the opposite end
of a hundred years, afraid
to step out onto that shadowy,
watery earth. A tree
ran its tentative fingers
over the spine of the roof.

At my feet, brass beads
from melted welding rods
lay scattered over the ground
like a broken necklace.
On the walls, I could see
hook, spike, and hinge,
flange, tong, and hammer
waiting. On a chair
tipped into a corner,
a bellows bound in cobwebs
fought hard for a breath.
It wanted to tell me.

Home Storage Barns

They're easy to see from the freeway,
backed into fences like cattle
and showing their ribs to the wind,
or standing up under the eaves
of a house, holding a dog on a chain—

little red valentine barns in which
scholarly spiders relax in their carrels,
having related one thing to another,
one year to the next, having tied all
the loose ends. Or there are those

unsold and still empty as barrels,
by the dozens in lumberyard lots,
waiting for someone who's wanted
a barn all his life that will fit
a small space in the present,

a barn of a reasonable scale,
yet that looks like a barn ought to look
to a person who's dreaming
(with an X of white boards on the door
as if marking a spot for the heart).

Surveyors

They have come from the past,
wearing their orange doublets
like medieval pages.

Seeing through time, they see
nothing of us. For them
the world is rock upon rock.

There is always the one
on one side of the highway,
holding his yellow staff,

and one on the other,
his one eye boring through
cars and trucks. It is as if

we were all invisible,
streaming between them
like ghosts, not snapping

the tightened string of light
they hold between them, nor
catching it across the bumper

and dragging them bouncing
behind us into our lives.
We mean nothing to them

in our waxed sedans, in our
business suits and fresh spring
dresses. They stand by the road

in the leaning grass, lifting
their heavy gloves of gold
to wave across the traffic,

and though they cannot see us,
helpfully we wave back.

4

A Stoneware Crock

Take hold of this old five-gallon crock
stamped with its little red wings,
and hook your thumbs over its lip,
and let it fly you back over the years

to the gray-green backwater valley
of pickles, to sugary kitchens
with galvanized buckets of cucumbers
smelling like freshly brushed hair,

a place of red hands, of oilcloth,
of mason jars bubbling in canners
enameled like midnight and spattered
with stars, of linoleum floors

where big women move on their casters
like upright pianos, rumbling along
with their bifocals steamed, keeping
the stove stoked, the coffeepot on,

their gossip rolling at a steady boil
as the packed jars cool, and lids clack in
upon the vacuum, and the morning air
is wild with flags of vinegar.

Aunt Mildred

After she'd cooked and then eaten the meat,
she washed and rinsed the butcher paper
under a pitcher pump that drew red water
up from a cistern under the house, rain
speckled with dirt from the cedar shingles,

then put the paper out on the line to dry,
using old clothespins whitened by lye
(the paper pinned next to her underthings,
which she dried inside her pillow cases
so they couldn't be seen from the street),

then pressed the paper with a hot sadiron
and carefully cut it into little squares,
picked up a pencil stub and pinched it hard,
straightened her spine, and wrote a small
but generous letter to the world.

Some Kinds of Love

On a warm June day,
four people push
a yellow plastic paddleboat
down a gravel road.

Above them, cottonwoods
rattle their shiny leaves.

A hundred feet ahead,
a rusty bridge
rides over ragweed
and a muddy creek.

The boat rides crazily
atop a child's red wagon,
squealing along
on wobbly wheels.

A plump red-headed boy,
flush-faced with laughter,
keeps the wagon in place
by scuttling along
in the yellow dust
and tugging its tongue.
His head thumps up against
the boat's blue bottom,
a drum for this parade.

A second, older boy
trots breathless at the front,
one hand steering the fat boat's
snout. His red cheeks shine
from all the screaming.
One of his shoes is untied.

Behind, a woman in shorts
and a halter-top
puts her hard white legs
into the work of pushing.
A sweep of hot red hair
spills over her face
as she yells down into the dust.

And, caressing the stern
with the touch of a pianist,
a man about the woman's age—
Down's syndrome, red hair—
follows stumbling along,
his broad face all drawn in
around a small wet smile.

A Ghost Story

Her life was plain, her death
a common death—a girl
sewn into the watery shroud
of pneumonia. She was only
another Mary, there
in Illinois, and it was only
another April—the buds
of the honeysuckle folded
in prayer. Forgotten eyes,
forgotten smile, the cowlick
in her hair forgotten;
everything gone. Yet for
seventy years her grave
gave off the scent of roses.

Another Story

In a country churchyard, two workmen
were digging a grave. It was summer,
but cool in the cedar-blue shade
of the white clapboard church where they labored.

Their picks did all of the talking.
Beyond them, a field of tall corn
glittered with heat, and above, a lone bird
rose on the air like an ash.

The grave grew slowly down
and out of the world, and the world rolled
under the work. Then the men stopped.
One stooped to scrape in the clay.

When he stood, light-headed,
swaying a little, he held in his hand
an old cowbell, covered with dirt
and packed with darkness.

He scraped out the earth with his knife.
The bell had no clapper. He shook it.
A meadowlark piped on a fence post.
In the distance, a feeder thunked.

He handed it across the grave
to the younger man, who held it in his hands
like a baby bird, then rang it tenderly.
A crow cawed in a cedar top.

He rang it again. On the highway,
a mile away, a semi trumpeted.
In the cornfield, an irrigation pump
thumped with a regular heartbeat.

He handed it back to the older man,
who set it aside. All afternoon,
they worked without a word between them.
At intervals each touched the empty bell.

In a Kitchen Garden

The seasons have learned to do lovely things
with an old plank path, cupping each board
so that on a morning in late July
each holds a thin reflecting pool of dew
dusted with hollyhock pollen.
Time has been set aside for the winter moon
to rub silver into the open grain,
and for the sun to bake each board as hard
as the lid of a grand piano,
so that a cane like this one, lifting
the cabbage leaves for Evelyn Penfield,
can make a kind of music there.

Nocturne

On the old man's face,
the gray moth of a mustache
spreads its soft wings,
a thing of dust and starlight,
scarcely stirring.

A bald head nods.
Blue hands
hang onto the flying chair.

The moth is the absolute color of time.

If it had eyes,
they would be tiny beads of blood.

Drawn there by a glimmer,
the wings fan out and leave a trace of dust
on the cooling, moist glass of the face.

5

Five Finger Exercise

All day at home, alone in the winter half-light,
I watched the wild birds feeding, coming and going,
their flight light as ashes over the yellow coals
of cracked corn, of millet and linnet seed.
And because of a darkness feeding in me, I saw
in bare branches the rags of a frock coat flying,
the charred pages of hymnals settling through smoke,
candle wax cooling, becoming the breast of a sparrow.
And as I waited there, five small black birds as quick
as quarter notes touched down at once, striking
a perfect chord at the cold, high end of the keyboard,
and it frightened them, and off they flew together.

Barn Owl

High in the chaffy, taffy-colored haze
of the hayloft, up under the starry
nail-hole twinkle of the old tin roof,
there in a nest of straw and baling twine
I have hidden my valentine for you:
a white heart woven of snowy feathers
in which wide eyes of welcome open
to you as you climb the rickety ladder
into my love. Behind those eyes is
a boudoir of intimate darkness, darling,
the silks of oblivion. And set like a jewel
dead center in the heart is a golden hook
the size of a finger ring, to hold you
always, plumpest sweetheart mouse of mine.

An Epiphany

I have seen the Brown Recluse Spider
run with a net in her hand, or rather,
what resembled a net, what resembled
a hand. She ran down the gleaming white floor
of the bathtub, trailing a frail swirl
of hair, and in it the hull of a beetle
lay woven. The hair was my wife's,
long and dark, a few loose strands, a curl
she might idly have turned on a finger,
she might idly have twisted, speaking to me,
and the legs of the beetle were broken.

Peeling a Potato

Pablo Casals should see me now,
bowing this fat little cello,
peeling off long white chords.

I am not famous like Pablo,
not yet. The amphitheater
of the kitchen sink is nearly empty.
As the notes reel out,
I hear only the hesitant clapping
of a few moist hands.

I am playing the solo variations
of J. S. Bach. Wonderfully,
I sweep with my peeler. See me lean
into the work, tight lipped,
the light in my hair. Inspiration
trickles over my handsome old hands.

The Mouse in the Piano

Hers (or is it his?) is a new
and remarkable music,
played out in the morning darkness
in the darker piano,
waking us up at two and then three
with those tentative notes
struck with mallets of straw
or the stems of leaves,
but not upon the strings themselves,
oh, no—upon the wooden case,
releasing the intimate chords
from the grain, a music
kept hidden there in secret
for more than a hundred years,
played now with perfect
concentration, but with little respect
for the old piano itself,
as if it were little more
than an apple barrel
or a bin for flour
through which the silvery strings—
a great abstraction
dumb and human—
fall all night like moonbeams
through the lifting dust.

Spider Eggs

In the shadows under the cellar stairs,
the fear of darkness, spinning there
all day with the steady whirr
of an old refrigerator, has formed
a solar system all its own:
five pea-size planets, slung in a web
of dust and frozen propane gas,
orbit the spark in a spider's skull—
too dense a head to let the light out
onto the clouds of dirty laundry—
but bright in its own black way
and pulling all the light in after it,
one fifty-watt bulb at a time.

A Statue of the Unknown Soldier

Because he was always to stand there
superior, high on his pedestal,
staring out over our heads from beneath
the stone bill of his watch cap;

and because at the feet of a statue
all people are children, diminished;
the sculptor foreshortened this soldier
and chiseled his head just a shade big

for his body. It must have made sense
in the studio, but perspective
is tricky; from the opposite side
of the street, from the point of view

of the mannequins jauntily lifting
their heels in the window of Penney's,
he looks like a child, his head too large
for the care-broken, delicate shoulders.

He is weary from walking so far
from the quarry, dragging his symbols:
his ragged Yankee uniform, his rifle
as thick as a fence post, this boy

with his lips pulled down over
a pout of bad teeth. He's a sad one,
all right, with a poor complexion;
over the years, his face has been stung

time and again by the smoke of blizzards
and pocked by the grapeshot of hail
whistling in over the five-and-dime.
Such action he's seen in his time:

those Shriners soft as marshmallows
riding their scooters, the high school bands
with trumpets that sound like someone
tearing up cotton for bandages, and worse,

those majorettes, every Fourth of July,
lifting a leg and kicking it once,
then lifting the other and kicking it too.
making it all look so terribly easy.

Stream Bed

In the poplars,
the hot rattle
of armies.

In the willows,
the whispers
of courtesans.

All is the same
each day
in the kingdom,

and the toad sets out
to market,
blinking.

6

A Sound in the Night

There's a clock at the end of the pasture,
tocking and tocking. It's my neighbor's new
electric fencer, a red tin box
with a steady pulse. On a night like this,
chilly and still, you can hear it knock
for a hundred yards, counting the stars
with its bony knuckle, a sound absurd
against the darkness. But many of us
have stopped in our places to listen:
a mouse with a globe of dew in her paws,
a coyote lifting his head from the grass,
his wet tail tipped with starlight.
Even my father, dead these fourteen years,
has heard the flat, remorseless counting,
and reaches out into the darkness
and over the years for my mother's hand.

For Jeff

On the morning of your wedding
I walked alone in the little park
where sometimes we ran and played
when you were small. My father
was living then and would walk
behind us as we jumped and laughed,
his step already cautious, his eyes
on his everyday wing-tip shoes
as they parted the grass. It was
as if he had begun to sense
that the world is less than solid,
for he stepped out so thoughtfully
onto each day: hands in his pockets,
jacket zipped to the neck,
his brown felt hat, brim up,
on the back of his head as if
a wind were blowing into his face,
and such a wind was surely blowing.

This time it was I who walked there,
buttoned against the wind, alone,
my hands in my jacket pockets,
a ball of Kleenex closed in one fist.
Under a spreading tree by a stream,
I shaded my eyes with my father's hand.
Through swirls of diamonds I saw you
run swiftly ahead, looking back
to encourage a boy with a kite
as he clumsily followed, tugging
the string. And as I watched
from my place at the back of your life,
the kite bounced along on its tail,
then shuddered and lifted itself,
and shook off its own surprise.

Sparklers

I scratched your name in longhand
on the night, then you wrote mine.
I couldn't see you, near me,
laughing and chasing my name
through the air, but I could hear
your heart, I think, and feel your breath
against the darkness, hurrying.

One word swirled out of your hand
as you rushed hard to write it
all the way out to its end
before its beginning was gone.
It left a frail red line
trembling along on the darkness,
and that was my name, my name.

Old Dog In March

From a cold stone stoop,
stepping down slowly
into another spring,

stretching his back,
stretching his back legs,
one leg at a time,

making a bridge
with his spine, reaching
from winter out and out,

forever out it seems,
then quaking at the end of it,
all down his length

so that his claws
skitter a little, losing
their grip on the world,

an old brown dog
gone stiff from chasing
all winter through dreams,

recovers his balance,
and, one ache at a time,
lowers himself

to the solid field of promise,
where with pink tip
of tongue between his teeth,

and frosty muzzle,
he sips the cool, delicious,
richly storied wind.

The Back Door

The door through which we step out
into the past is an easy push,
light as the air, a green screen door
with a sagging spring. There's a hook
to unhook first, for there have been
incidents: someone has come up
out of the past to steal something good
from the present. We know who they are.
We have tried to discourage them
by moving from house to house,
from city to city, but they find us
again and again. You see them coming
sometimes from a long ways off—
a pretty young woman, a handsome man,
stepping in through the back garden gate,
pausing to pick the few roses.

The Great Grandparents

As small children, we were taken to meet them.
They had recently arrived from another world
and stood dumbfounded in the busy depot
of the present, their useless belongings in piles:
old tools, old words, old recipes, secrets.
They searched our faces and grasped our hands
as if we could lead them back, but we drew them
forward into the future, feeling them tremble,
their shirt cuffs yellow, smoky old wood stoves
smoldering somewhere under their clothes.

A Good-bye Handshake

Though you and the nursing home
are miles behind me now, your hand
with its dark blue age spots
is here in my hand, your fingers warm

from all of the hot steel handles
they held in your eighty-eight years—
levers of threshing machines,
of sickle-bar mowers and balers—

but cooling now and slowly going
all blue-black over brown, like a pool
of blue oil on the floor of a barn,
that darkness working its way up

into the cuff of your new plaid shirt,
up past your elbow, sharp as a plowshare
there on the wheelchair armrest,
easing over your heart like a shadow.

A hundred miles down the road, stopped by
the highway and sitting in shade
at the edge of a shimmering cornfield,
I say good-bye. I am headed both farther

and further than you, Ira Friedlein.
With love I take your blue-black hand,
which has held nearly everything once
and has squeezed it shyly and politely.

The Sweeper

It is morning. My father
in shirtsleeves is sweeping
the sidewalk in front of his store,
standing up straight in the bow
of his gondola, paddling
the endless gray streets of his life
with an old yellow oar—
happy there, hailing his friends.

7

Weather Central

Each evening at six-fifteen, the weatherman
turns a shoulder to us, extends his hand,
and talking softly as a groom, cautiously
smooths and strokes the massive, dappled flank
of the continent, touching the cloudy whorls
that drift like galaxies across its hide,
tracing the loops of harness with their barbs
and bells and pennants; then, with a horsefly's touch,
he brushes a mountain range and sets a shudder
running just under the skin. His bearing
is cavalier from years of success and he laughs
at the science, yet makes no sudden moves
that might startle that splendid order
or loosen the physics. One would not want to wake
the enormous Appaloosa mare of weather,
asleep in her stall on a peaceful moonlit night.

Ted Kooser

was born in Ames, Iowa, in 1939. He was educated in the Ames public schools, at Iowa State University, and the University of Nebraska. His awards include two National Endowment for the Arts Fellowships, the Stanley Kunitz Prize from *Columbia* magazine, and the 1981 Society of Midland Authors Award for Poetry for *Sure Signs*. His poems have appeared in many magazines including, most recently, *The Antioch Review, The Hudson Review,* and *The Kenyon Review*. He lives on an acreage near Garland, Nebraska, and makes his living as a life insurance executive. He is also an adjunct professor at the University of Nebraska where he teaches occasional courses in poetry writing.